Far From Easy

What It Takes to Make Your Dreams a Reality

RICKY ROBERTS III

IP INDEPENDENTLY PUBLISHED

Far From Easy
Copyright © 2019 by Ricky Roberts III. All rights reserved.

This book is designed to provide accurate and authoritative information with regard to the subject matter covered. This information is given with the understanding that the author is not engaged in rendering legal or professional advice. Since the details of your situation are fact dependent, you should seek additional services of a competent professional.

Cover Design: Keith Burnson
Editor: Jeanie Lyubelsky
Bio Photo: Joey Clay ©

Published in the United States of America
1. Self-Help / Dreams
2. Self-Help / Happiness
19.04.24

CONTENTS

Introduction   7

Willingness   11

Acting on Your Dreams   15

Devotion   20

Sacrifice   26

Clarity   29

Work   34

Be Committed   39

Courage   42

Mental Strength   45

Belief   49

Trust the Process   53

Patience   57

Struggle   62

Self-Care   68

Stay in Your Lane   71

Closing Thoughts   74

Far
From
Easy

INTRODUCTION

The ideas and terms that are thrown around loosely regarding the pursuit of your dreams, generally speaking, fall short in expressing the actions necessary to make them your reality. I have certainly been guilty of using terms that give no real value to dream seekers. Although some words may offer a short-lived sense of inspiration and motivation, they fall short of explaining what it means to pursue your dreams and ultimately make them your reality. Pursuing your dreams is more complex than any cliché, statement, or phrase that people, including myself, might say in an attempt to encourage others.

Beyond catchy phrases, the many different social media channels from which we consume information, guidance, and inspiration tend to create a glorified version of what it means to act on your dreams. We often see the results—but not the truth behind what it takes to get them. Furthermore, even people currently living them to some extent generally only show the highlights, successes, and progress, and I am guilty of this too. On top of the glamorous perspective we see, we are sold steps, habits, and keys, as if we can magically achieve our dreams with these answers. This is not to say that some books, workshops, seminars, and courses are not helpful and worth seeking out for knowledge and insight. I know that I have benefited, and still do, from many great teachers, authors, speakers, YouTube channels, and podcasts. They have brought, and still bring, value to my life in one way or another. Having said that, I am not attempting to discredit or minimize anyone's efforts to inspire others to pursue their dreams. If positive content is made with good intentions, we can never have enough of it.

However, there is more to making your dreams a reality than inspirational phrases, steps to follow, and believing in the law of attraction. The purpose of this book is to give you a real vision of pursuing your dreams, not one that will just make you feel excited in the moment, which eventually fades over time anyway. My intention is to inspire and support you on your journey while also being realistic about what you will encounter along the way. The focus is to equip you with an understanding of what you need, and things you will go through in the process, to make your dreams a reality.

People give up on their dreams for various reasons. I believe that some of them are related to false ideas people have about how things are supposed to go, how quickly they should happen, and a lack of awareness about how hard the pursuit gets along the way.

We have all heard stories about people being so close to giving up on their dreams from getting discouraged by the many struggles they faced—before their dreams materialized. The struggle is real and so is the joy you get when you rise above it all.

I believe whole-heartedly that with attention and taking the right steps, you have everything it takes to make your dreams a reality. I hope this book will be a small piece of the puzzle that helps you along the way.

WILLINGNESS

If I had to pinpoint any one thing that was at the start of pursuing my own dreams, and realizing them to the extent that I have so far, it is willingness. Before anything in the rest of this book will be relevant, you must determine how willing you really are to create the life of your dreams. Please answer the questions that follow. Be completely honest with yourself. Also, if you are already on the pursuit of your dreams, or living them to any extent, the questions are still equally as important to answer. In fact, they will help you check in with your own purposeful progress.

Are you willing to listen to your heart enough to truly identify your dreams?

Are you willing to actively move toward achieving your dreams? Even when you are not getting paid, recognized, appreciated, supported, or encouraged…?

Are you willing to sacrifice and let go of your own ideas about how you want the pursuit to go and the exact time frames in which you want things to happen?

Are you willing to be so devoted to your dreams that you will do whatever it takes to make them your reality?

Are you willing to be so committed that you will not let anything—or anyone—deter or distract you?

Are you willing to ignore your own lack of belief that you may have and every other naysayer that doubts you?

Are you willing to keep going when you feel defeated, you're broke (mentally, emotionally, or financially), and you don't seem to be getting anywhere?

Are you willing to have unwavering faith in your dream—no matter what happens or what others say about you?

Are you willing to trust yourself and the purpose of your dreams, even when there is no obvious evidence that you should?

Are you willing to remain patient when you're five years, ten years, or even further along into your pursuit, and yet your dreams still seem so far away?

Are you willing to ask for, and accept, help?

Are you willing to struggle—not just a little bit—but a lot?

Are you willing to let go of certain relationships that are holding you back, possessions you don't necessarily need, and the idea of "job security?"

Are you willing to face your greatest fears and insecurities?

Are you willing to go 'all in' on your dreams? Not just talking about them or pretending to pursue them, but going all in on them; in other words, is making your dreams become a reality the *only* option and plan for you?

Be brutally honest with yourself when answering the questions in this section. Take some time to reflect on each one. Read them multiple times. Put yourself in different scenarios with each question and ask, "Am I willing?"

Making your dreams a reality is not just a specific place you end up or a list of things you achieve. It's much more than that. It is a process that is forever expanding, and the exact details of getting to the destination are always changing. Eventually over time, what was once a pursuit becomes your dreams realized—through the life you live every day, because you are acting on the things that make you feel a sense of fulfillment and joy like nothing else can. This is a life-long pursuit. Chances are that you will accomplish so much more than you originally set out to do with the dreams and visions of your heart.

If you answered 'yes' to each question I posed in this section, then you have what it takes to make your dreams a reality. In truth, we all have this drive in us, but not everyone is willing to do what it takes to make it all happen. Now that you have agreed that you are ready, let's dive a little deeper into what it takes.

ACTING ON YOUR DREAMS

Your dreams are a part of you. They will never be silenced, no matter how much you ignore them. Even if you spend your whole life ignoring them—and live a good life doing so—they will not leave you. They will always tug on your heart, waiting for you to act on their call in your life.

One thing that keeps people from making their dreams a reality is action. Taking action is the only thing that will give your dreams a chance to manifest into reality. You can tell everyone you know about your dreams and even write them down, but if you don't pursue them, they are just dreams.

Some required actions may not be fun and may be extremely scary, but that cannot stop you. Some of them will be bold and will seem paramount to your pursuit. These are great and much needed. However, know that the actions you take on a daily basis are equally important.

The compilation of small actions day in and day out are crucial. You cannot just identify a handful of big actions and expect your dreams to automatically become your reality. Although they may offer you short-term gains or a sense of achievement, reaching your dreams will require ongoing, daily actions. From the moment you acknowledge your willingness to face everything necessary to pursue them, you will need to take actions on your dreams daily. Each step does not need to be massive. It's the small things you do regularly that play a huge role in making progress. As long as you do at least one thing each day that relates to your dreams, your efforts will turn into a collection of actions that will eventually move you closer to success. This is not a sprint; it's a life-long journey. The massive actions are still important and very much necessary, but don't get so overwhelmed by them that you end up not taking any action at all.

Consider, for example: If the only thing I thought about when pursuing my dreams as an author was the final stages of publishing my books and how to spread the word about them, which takes a combination of several big actions, I would probably never write a book. I would get so overwhelmed by the publishing and marketing processes that I would more than likely never start.

I often get asked by people thinking about writing a book, "How do I get a book published?" My answer is, "Start writing the book. Don't worry about who will read it or how you will publish it—focus on writing it first. When that happens, then you will figure out the rest." The one thing that gets me to the point of releasing any book is writing, even just a few pages, every day. On most days, what I am writing about has nothing to do with a specific book I am working on, but I still write and keep taking small daily actions toward my dreams as a full-time author. Eventually, I get to the place where I have a draft, and it becomes time to move on to the bigger actions necessary to make my manuscript available for others to read. Over time, with months of writing sessions in my journals on a daily basis, my written words become a book.

The actions do not always have to involve your dreams directly, per se. Your daily actions may include a variety of things that are somehow centered on practicing your craft. For example, you might listen to podcasts or watch interviews that showcase other people living their dreams. You may want to spend time reflecting on, meditating about, and visualizing your dreams becoming reality. Talk about them or write them out in detail. Whatever you do, take some type of action toward them—daily. Since everyone's dreams can be so different, the actions that you take will be as well. Furthermore, only you will know if you are doing them or not. If most of the actions you need to take seem like they are all huge tasks, don't get discouraged. Break them down into smaller actions that you can work on every day. Eventually, the small actions will turn into accomplishing the big things that once seemed so daunting.

Also, keep in mind that there will be days, at some point, in which the actions you are taking are actually a part of your dreams being realized. For example, if I want to be a speaker and am practicing speaking in front of a large audience, I am acting on my dreams while experiencing them being realized at the same time.

Whenever you get any type of traction, acknowledgment, or sense of momentum, then stop, reflect, and take the time to celebrate your progress. This is very important to do, because there will be hundreds, if not thousands, of actions that you will take that will feel like they are nothing for getting you closer to your dreams and are yielding no results. Don't worry—even tiny steps are important, and they are all a part of your dreams manifesting into reality. When you celebrate moments of progress, you are also honoring the many small actions you took to make them possible—even the ones that you felt were not helping.

The actions you take, or don't, on your dreams will determine whether or not you make your dreams come true.

DEVOTION

The level of devotion you have to pursue your dreams must be unwavering. When things get overwhelming, discouraging, and painful, you are being tested. If you are not fully devoted, and if you are at all flexible on whether or not you will make your dreams a reality, then when those tests come, chances are that you will want to abandon your pursuit. You cannot be devoted only after you have read an inspiring book, watched an uplifting YouTube video, or attended a conference. You must remain devoted even when everything seems to be crumbling around you, you're almost out of money, you feel more alone and isolated than ever, and you are questioning yourself and your dreams. Every time you rise above the turbulent times on your pursuit, you will build even more confidence in yourself and in the belief of your dreams being realized.

Pursuing your dreams is not easy. It's important for you to devote yourself fully to them. You cannot go into it with a plan B or C. There is only one plan, and that plan is for you to make your dreams a reality. When you have a back-up plan, then the level of your devotion will waiver in times of distress. If that happens, you are more likely to find multiple excuses as to why you should give up on your dreams and create many stories in your head to justify doing so.

In the same way, I asked you a variety of questions to gauge your willingness to pursue your dreams, I will ask you similar questions again for you to check in with yourself on how devoted you really are. Asking yourself these questions helps to fully embrace, and anchor yourself into, the level of devotion you need to make your dreams a reality.

On a scale of one to ten, how devoted are you to making your dreams a reality?

Are you devoted enough to never give up, no

matter how hard it gets?

Are you devoted enough to downsize and simplify your lifestyle if need be?

Are you devoted enough to sell things and let go of things that you don't need… and possibly some things you think you may need?

When necessary, are you devoted enough to go without certain luxuries you may be used to enjoying?

Are you devoted enough to ignore all of the people that will tell you to stick with your job or career plan instead of pursuing your dreams?

Are you devoted enough to believe in your dreams no matter how many voices, including the ones in your own head, are telling you not to?

Are you devoted enough to give up the idea of certainty and security for a path that is completely unknown and has no guarantees?

These questions are based on the reality of what you will encounter on your journey of making your dreams a reality. These questions are not presented to scare you. They are meant to help you prepare by being realistic with how devoted you actually need to be in order to make your dreams a reality. I can personally attest to all of them.

When I decided to go all in on my dreams and be completely devoted to them, I had to let go of a lot. Things got tough. There were times when I had no clue about how I was going to make it. I just knew that giving up was not an option. I was, and still am, all in, completely devoted and willing to go as far as necessary to make my dreams a reality. Books weren't selling, and I wasn't getting many paid speaking engagements at the time. I continued to practice speaking voluntarily, and I sold pretty much every material thing I could to keep things going while even having to get help to buy groceries. Being someone who experienced poverty on many levels in my childhood, I had always promised myself that I would never be poor again. To end up in that place while pursuing something so important and necessary to me was truly challenging. I questioned myself and everything I believed about my dreams. I had to humble myself greatly and stay focused on what it was all for—continually reaching toward my dreams. I wasn't broke at the time because I wasn't capable of getting a good job; it was because giving up on my dreams wasn't an option. My mind was made up. I had to keep going.

In those times, I experienced some of my greatest

challenges. I fought with depression nearly every day, and my mind was consumed with doubt. Beyond my internal struggles, I had friends suggesting all of the things I could do, or jobs I could get, to make money. They didn't get it, and knowing that made things even worse. I knew I had to give all of my time and attention to writing, marketing the books I had out at the time, and building my speaking network. If I did not continue to pour myself into my dreams as much as I had been back then, I know they would have never happened. I am so grateful that I didn't fold. Deep down, I always knew it was all just a matter of time before things would start to work out better, which proved, and continues to prove, to be true.

There are so many people that start down a tough and sometimes lonely path toward realizing their dreams, and unfortunately many of them give up when things get rough. When the glamorized version of pursuing their dreams becomes the reality of the effort it takes, they are not devoted enough to keep going. They don't give up because they are not capable or worthy, they give up because they were never devoted enough in the first place.

Gauge the truth about the depth of your devotion.

Be honest with yourself. Either you're devoted enough, or you're not. If you're not, there is nothing wrong with you. It doesn't make you any less of a person. However, if you are, you will make it through whatever challenges lie ahead on your journey. When you are fully devoted to your dreams, nothing will keep you from making them your reality.

SACRIFICE

The things you will have to sacrifice for your dreams will change continuously. One moment it may involve not doing something you love, or spending time with friends and family, and the next it may be getting a cheaper car or downsizing your home. You may have to avoid buying any new clothes for a while, not get the latest gadgets, or hold off on taking a trip that you really want to go on. If you are serious about your plan, then whatever your sacrifices are, they're all worth it.

There were many trips that I didn't go on, events or

outings with friends I missed, concerts I didn't attend, things I went without—including not having a car at one point—to keep the pursuit of my dreams alive. The sacrifices I made, and still make when necessary, are nothing compared to the happiness I experience from living my dreams.

There will be so many things you want to do but can't, or shouldn't, if you are serious about making your dreams a reality. There will be moments when you question if it is all worth it and if you're even getting closer to living your dreams anyway. Everyone around you will appear, at times, like they have it all figured out. The path they are choosing to go down, even though it is not the pursuit of their dreams, may start to look more attractive. The opportunities they have to buy certain things and to go on exciting trips may seem worth ignoring your dreams in order to have them too. Eventually, you may even consider giving up on your dreams to buy into the life they live—even if not a single one of them lives their own dream.

Sacrificing things that will give you short-term satisfaction now may start to seem less appealing the more you do it. Doing it a few times may not be bad at all, but after ten times, one hundred times, or even more, it gets harder. As much as it gets more difficult at times, it will also get easier. Every time you make a sacrifice for your dreams, you are confirming to yourself how serious you are about them and that nothing will hold you back. Over time with making your dreams a priority, the belief you have in them will continue to strengthen. Beyond reinforcing your growing belief system, you will also see little gains along the way that will remind you it is all worth it. Choices you make that seems like sacrifices now, those which you know in your heart are moving you in the direction of your dreams, are more than worth it.

Important Consideration:
Please do not confuse sacrificing for your dreams with not doing anything for yourself or for—and with—your loved ones. As important as it is to sacrifice some of the short-term pleasures of the present to create your dream life in the future, it is also important for you to enjoy daily life and the process of making your dreams a reality along the way.

CLARITY

There is no clear and easy path to living your dreams. In fact, your specific situation and where you want to be may mean that your journey will be one of a kind. You will be carving out your new road with many turns, some of which will be wrong. You will have to find ways around detours, roadblocks, and setbacks. Although there is often no preset direction that you need to follow in order to make your dreams a reality, you will need clarity on what it all means to you.

What do you want your life to be? In other words, what is the most accurate vision of your dreams? Your first response to those questions may be that you know exactly what your vision is—what you want to be or what specific business you want to open.

Now, I want to ask you again a little differently. This time I invite you to think about your answer in great detail and depth. What do you truly and deeply dream of your life being? Not just what you want to do, start, or what you think you want your life to be based on what you may think is expected of you in the area of your chosen dreams. What kind of lifestyle do you really want? What does living life on your terms look like? Getting clear on what your dreams are in their fullness will help you stay focused and avoid the temptation of doing things that are not authentic to you, only because you feel obligated to doing them.

In my space of living my dream as an author and speaker, there is pressure and some level of expectation to have a podcast, YouTube channel, online courses, and more, all of which do not feel authentic to me. I am not particularly excited by the idea of doing any of them, at least not now. I don't see any of them as a part of what it looks like for me to continue living the life of my dreams. This is not to say that I don't see the benefit in all of them from certain perspectives, because I do.

For me, it comes down to doing what feels right and if it aligns with the clarity I have of how I want my life to be, or not. Unless I feel authentically moved to do something, I will not do it. This isn't just a career for me—it's me living the life of my dreams. What feels best for me will ultimately facilitate me in giving my best to others.

This is in no way to say that if everything isn't easy and fun, then don't do it. Everything great you do will require putting in the work to learn and become comfortable. It's the authentic desire to do what needs to be done that makes the hard stuff manageable versus miserable. Being clear helps you stay in tune with what feels right and what doesn't. If a task or direction is not right for you, then don't do it just because you feel like you should. You will know the difference.

For me, doing podcasts, having a YouTube channel, and hosting online trainings could very likely fit into the vision of someone's dream of being an author and speaker, which is amazing. There are many authors and speakers that I respect and admire that do all of these things, and do them well, which I am grateful for because of the value they bring to my life and those of others. They seem to work beautifully for them, as such activities could for others that see them as part of their dreams.

What I want to share with you is that I am clear on what the reality of my dreams looks like, and I am living them. If I wasn't clear on the overall lifestyle I envision for myself, it would be easy to do things that don't feel right to me, because I would think they are a part of what is required of me to reach my dreams. By doing them, they will not bring me closer to my dreams; they will actually distract me from living them.

Not doing certain things is not about the unwillingness to work through not liking them, not being good at them, or having to spend the time to learn them; it is about those activities not fitting authentically into the vision of my dreams. When I went all in on my dreams, I set out to live a life of freedom, being in charge of my days and how I spend them, while impacting and inspiring others through my books and speaking engagements. The other stuff is not a part of that vision, at least not yet.

One of my main focuses is to live a life doing things I love and to have the time to enjoy the life I create for myself. This does not mean that I don't get slightly distracted by ideas of doing things that don't align fully with my dreams. I have, and I imagine I will again in the future. If I wasn't clear on what living my dreams looks like for me, I could easily dim my passion and focus by giving my time and energy to things that don't inspire me, just because I think I need to do them. My dreams are not about what I need to do, they are about what I feel called to do. That is what I act on, and I encourage you to do the same.

Be clear on your dreams. What that looks like today may change. That is okay. The important thing is to keep checking in with yourself, so you remain connected to the truth in the vision of your dreams, not what you think they should be because of pressure or others' opinions. Whatever that vision is, revisit it often and see it as your reality. If you're already living it, keep at it and stay true to yourself.

WORK

I often sense that people love the idea of what it means to pursue their dreams but not the truth about what it takes to make them a reality. I have witnessed countless people talk about the ideas of their dreams and even dabble in pursuing them part time while still working at their 'day job.' Beginning the pursuit of your dreams while still working a job with a guaranteed income is not a bad idea. However, at some point, you have to take the leap to go all in on your dreams rather than only working on them in your spare time. Otherwise, they will not be fully realized. When you make that leap is up to you, but at some point, it has to be done.

I have seen people go all in on their dreams but quickly give up when they realize what it actually takes to make them happen, which can be outright disheartening. Beyond that, even though people may understand the work involved, they are not always willing to do it, especially when there is so much of it that does not bring compensation or reward on any level for a long time.

Pursuing your dreams requires late nights and early mornings. In many ways, when it is your dreams you are manifesting—through action into reality—the work never stops. As the pursuit becomes your life, there is no division between the two. When you are acting on your dreams, you are not working in the typical sense of the word... the situation is better defined as your life's work. There is a difference. In other words, there is no start at 9 a.m., take a lunch break, and get off at 5 p.m. when you are living on the path of your dreams. Regardless of whether or not you are physically acting on them in the moment, you will essentially work on your dreams 24/7—as they are always on your mind. This is your life's work, not just a job you do to pay the bills.

Although it is necessary to spend quality time with your loved ones, working on your dreams doesn't always stop when you do. When you are all in on your dreams, they can call you in to work at any time, and anywhere. Your loved ones will understand that about you, or maybe not. Either way, when your dreams call, you answer.

If I am on a vacation to get a break and I get inspired to write, I honor that call and go to work on my dreams. Even if it is as simple as taking a few minutes to write down the ideas that come to me, I will not ignore them. It's not about putting work in front of my down time or people I may be with at the time; it's about me realizing my dreams in their fullness as being an active part of every aspect of my life. They are not a burden or distraction to my life; rather, they are a source of great fulfillment in it. My dreams don't warrant separation, because they bring me joy, and I love not only living them but the continued process of realizing them in their fullness. From time to time, I intentionally disconnect from doing anything specific about my dreams and take time for self-care every day, but even then, on some level, I am still working on my dreams.

It is not one particular thing that you do that

defines working on your dreams; it is everything you do. Every choice you make in your life, on one level or another, is either taking you closer to or further away from realizing them.

Writing when I am inspired to do so, even if I am on a trip, always makes me happy. However, the times I am reading through a book for the twentieth time before it is released, when I spend hours on emails and scheduling logistics for speaking engagements, or I need to work out details for large book orders are not always enjoyable. The joy comes in knowing that it is all part of living my dreams and all therefore worth it. Even when I don't feel like carrying out such details, I am always grateful for them to continue living the life of my dreams.

There will be many things that are a part of making your dreams a reality that will not involve what you necessarily like doing. Yes, you can pay people to do certain things, but I believe even in that case, there will always be tasks that you do not prefer to, and cannot, delegate. It's okay. It's all part of the process. Whether you are on a vacation or you have to do the required things that you don't want to do, keep on working and do them anyway. Find fulfillment in knowing that you are working to make your dreams a reality and be grateful for all tasks that are a part of the process.

How many times have you heard someone who is working their job respond to the question, "How is your day going?" with, "It will be better when I get off of work"…? When you are pursuing your dreams, or living them, there is no 'getting off.' The amazing thing is that no matter how hard it gets, or how tired you become, you never feel like "you will be better when you get off." Your life is already better, because you are making your dreams a reality. No matter what the outcome is, or when your dreams start to become realized, there is no greater work that you can be doing than making your dreams a reality.

BE COMMITTED

B eing one foot in and one foot out for your dreams will not work. You have to be fully committed to them. When things get hard, and they will, stopping cannot be an option. The only option from your perspective is to keep pursuing your dreams—no matter what. You will need a non-negotiable level of commitment to make you dreams a reality. If you are not committed whole-heartedly, you will eventually fold under the process, struggles, setbacks, and challenges that accompany the pursuit of your dreams. On the other hand, the depth of your commitment will carry you through.

Unfortunately, I have seen many people work on their dreams for a while only to give up on them completely—or only pursue them partially before quitting. It was certainly not because they didn't, or don't, have the desire, talent, passion, or potential to make them come true. It is because they acted on them without being all in. They had back-up plans. Quitting became an option when the fantasy of what they thought following their dreams was going to be like became the reality of what it really is, which is not nearly as easy as they may have envisioned.

The level of commitment at which you pursue your dreams is up to you. There is absolutely nothing wrong with being slightly committed to your dreams. Enjoy it. Have fun dabbling in the idea of pursuing them. Even experiencing a glimpse of living your dreams is better than nothing at all.

On the other hand, if you want to see your dreams realized in their entirety, you will need to be fully committed to them. Make up your mind that nothing will distract you, and you will let nothing hold you back—not even yourself. Giving up cannot be an option no matter how difficult it gets, how frustrated or upset you become, or how many times you feel like you aren't making any progress. Your unwavering commitment will push you when you can't push yourself. Do not get distracted by having options or an alternative plan; know what your dreams are and commit to them for a lifetime.

Being fully committed is the only way you will be able to get through the thoughts, feelings, experiences, and criticisms (from yourself and others) that will make you want to stop. When you allow stopping to be an option, it will eventually become more attractive as time passes, and your mind will find hundreds of reasons to justify quitting. Giving up on your dream has nothing to do with whether or not you want it badly enough or how capable you are, but it has everything to do with being so committed that quitting is not an option.

COURAGE

Staring into the eyes of those you love and seeing doubt when you speak of your dreams is hard. Hearing the many reasons why what you want for your life won't work out from people around you (family, friends, and colleagues), watching informative but negative videos on YouTube, and reading about challenges in books and on blogs can be disheartening. You will hear about how hard your chosen path is, that you should consider something different instead, and eventually you may question if pursing your dreams is a practical and responsible thing to do.

Beyond the lack of belief from others, you will face your own self-doubt and criticism. In fact, you may even question your own sanity. There were certainly times early in the pursuit of my dreams that I questioned if I was a bit delusional, because I believed that I could make my dreams a reality. Some people around me, or even people I had just met, would express concerns when they saw how committed I was and what I was willing to let go of, and go through, in order to accomplish my objectives.

If you are not courageous for your dreams, what you have to face in order to live them will scare you away from acting on them. Fortunately, we all have the power to choose courage over fear. Do not be afraid of what you will encounter along the way. Whatever obstacles, challenges, and struggles you experience, you will overcome them.

There will be people that doubt you, put you down, and even encourage you... to give up. Be courageous and face their doubt as well as your own. No matter how intense it gets, lean into your courage and believe that you are capable and worthy of living the life of your dreams.

There is a reason the calling in your heart is so

strong. It will not go away, no matter how hard you try. Trust me; I tried for nearly ten years to ignore the tug on my heart to pursue my passion to inspire others. During that time, I had done well in the car business, chasing the idea that money would solve my problems and make me happy. I kept busy while buying cars, jewelry, and expensive clothes to justify not answering the call. Nothing I did to ignore it worked. Eventually, I answered, and I haven't turned back since.

Don't ignore your dreams. Embrace them and be courageous enough to make them your reality.

MENTAL STRENGTH

You can be the strongest person in the world physically, but it doesn't mean that you have the mental strength to realize your dreams. Although being healthy and physically strong is important, you will also need to be strong in the mind. You will need to withstand the negative self-talk, excuses, fears, and countless reasons why you're not worthy or capable of living your dreams. Your mental strength will keep you going when you can't sleep or eat because you're so discouraged and the only thing you feel like doing is giving up.

In order to have a strong mind, you will need to take good care of it. If you feed it with negativity, violence, fear, unproductive criticism, and allow it to take on the doubt of others—as well as your own—seriously, your thoughts will be weak. The negativity can consume your mind and will be at the forefront of where you are trying to go. Your thoughts can have you believing you are not worthy, not good enough, and that your dreams are crazy. Furthermore, if your mind is too weak to ignore all of the naysayers, you will start to believe their lies. You may even eventually be convinced to give up, which would be a horrible thing to do.

Master your mind, or it will master you. If you don't have enough mental strength to keep pursuing your dreams and overcoming the many challenges you will face along the way, your mind will talk you into settling for a life that can never make you happy—no matter how hard you try to convince yourself that it will. Your mind can make you believe that the dreams you have are not possible anyway, at least not for you. The more control you have over your mind with a healthy mindset, the greater chance you will have to make your dreams a reality.

Pay attention to the stories that are playing in your

mind. What is your self-talk like? What type of stories or dialogue does your mind produce on a regular basis? Are they healthy, positive, and encouraging? The more aware you are of your weaknesses, the easier they are to address.

As with anything that you want to make strong, it takes a lot of time and effort. Spend time exercising your mind by challenging it to learn new things. Read empowering, insightful, and positive material. Recite positive affirmations. Correct negative thoughts and limited beliefs the moment you have them. Fill your mind with as much inspiring content as you can. When you are driving, exercising, or spending time at home, listen to stuff that is good for you. Start paying attention to the conversations you have, and with whom you have them. Assess whether or not they are strengthening your mind by filling it with more positivity or weakening it with negativity.

When you begin to pay more attention to your thoughts and the things that you are allowing to come into your mind, it may surprise you how much negativity you are consuming on a regular basis. Negativity contributes to a weak mindset, while positivity helps facilitate a strong one. You decide which life you create for yourself by what you put into your mind and how active you are at changing, and letting go of, the thoughts that are not good for you.

This is not to say when you develop a strong mindset that you will never have negative thoughts again. However, the stronger your mindset is, the less likely you are to be controlled by any negative thoughts that do come up.

The world around you may say your dreams will never happen, and that you should give up. Maybe you won't feel like getting out of bed in the morning, you can't seem to handle the stress anymore, and you begin thinking you were wrong that you deserve to live your dreams in the first place.

Instead, you can train your brilliant and beautiful mind. You can strengthen it to remind you of just how worthy you are, how far you have already come, and that giving up is not an option—at least not for you.

A weak mind will tell you to quit, but a strong one will encourage you to keep pushing on—one day at a time—no matter how hard it gets.

BELIEF

As I mentioned earlier, not everyone will believe in your dreams. There is no reason to fault the people who don't. The truth is, in most cases, they have never believed in their own dreams nor had anyone else believe in them, so it's hard for them to believe in yours. You don't need them to believe in your dreams in order to make them your reality anyway.

It is nice to have people believe in your dreams, and it would be great if the people that didn't, did; but ultimately, the only belief that you can rely on and need is the belief you have in the life you were meant to live. Even the people who do believe in your dreams can change. At one point in time, they may believe, but as time passes and your dreams are not realized yet, their belief may diminish. Whether people believe in your dreams for one year, five years, or never at all, you cannot let it impact the belief you have in yourself.

How much do you truly believe in your dreams?

Do you believe in your dreams enough to keep going when no one else believes in them?

Do you believe in your dreams enough to get back up, time after time, when the obstacles you face bring you down?

Do you believe in your dreams enough to not give up, even when the people you care about most tell you that you should?

Do you believe in your dreams so much that even when you lose your motivation and feel like you can't go any further, you still believe anyway?

Do you believe in your dreams enough to silence the chatter in your mind telling you to give up on your dreams, you will never make it, you are not deserving enough, and that dreams are not for people like you (or where you come from, the family you grew up in, the background you have, etc.)?

Do you believe in your dreams enough to push on when you barely have money to eat (i.e., you may even need to ask for help to get food), you don't know how you will pay your bills, and you have to sell some of your possessions to keep your pursuit alive?

Read through each of those questions several times. Go deep within and reflect on each scenario. Imagine yourself in situations similar to what the questions describe, either ones you have been in already on your pursuit or could be in now. If you have already gone through some of them at this point in your pursuit, then tap into what it took for you to rise above and recall the level of belief you had to keep going. If you haven't been in any of the circumstances yet, anchor into the knowing that you have what it takes to get through the hard times when they arise. When everything feels like it's falling down around you, and people, including yourself, are telling you how unlikely you are to realize your dreams, it is your belief in them that will keep you going.

The belief I have in my dreams has been challenged many times. I faced fears, battled insecurities, and self-doubt—lots of it. I fell, have been knocked down, failed, made mistakes, got distracted, and have been in places where I had absolutely no idea how I would pay my bills. I was on food assistance from the Department of Children and Families. I had foreclosed on a house and filed for bankruptcy. I felt paralyzed by depression, and I was drained, confused, and afraid. The list goes on. But, no matter what happened or how badly I felt at any one time, I never stopped believing in my dreams.

Sure, it is easy to believe in your dreams when you talk about them, put them on your vision board, or write them down somewhere. The ideas of your dreams are exciting, and it is easy to feel really good about them. And, when you feel good, it is easy to say that you believe in them. You will need to not only believe in your dreams intellectually and philosophically, but you will need to believe in them whole-heartedly—with deep conviction—and without a shadow of a doubt. Your belief must be so strong that nothing will make it go away.

Believe that you can, you must, and you will make your dreams a reality.

TRUST THE PROCESS

The first edition of my first book, *YOU*, was released in 2004. This happened when I knew absolutely nothing about the publishing industry, or about being an author. Because of my lack of experience I thought, "This is it; once the book comes out, I will reach millions of people, sell millions of books, get interviewed by Oprah, and travel the world talking about it." That is not at all how it works.

When I released my first book, I was an unknown author and had no existing platform (although there was not significant social media at the time, there were blogs, email lists, and such, which I didn't have). The only people that I had to share my book with directly were my friends and family. I also had several book signings at different Barnes and Nobles locations to spread awareness, but the book quickly ran out of momentum shortly after the initial push. There were no news channels lining up to interview me, despite the media outlets my publisher at the time had reached out to. It didn't matter how important I thought my book was and how much I thought it would inspire people.

Within one month after it came out, I saw very quickly that the ideas I had about the book industry and what it meant to be a published author was not even close to reality. I thought once I released a book, everything else would happen magically. What I didn't know was that releasing my first book was only the start to a long and treacherous, but at the same time beautiful, process.

Yes, it is long. It is treacherous. But... it is also amazing. It is a process. The key is to trust in it. Trust that whatever you face along the way is all part of it. (If you are making one bad choice after another and not giving it your best efforts, which is causing your challenges, that is a completely different conversation to have). Trust that no matter how many troubles you face or what challenging detours you experience along the way, they are all working for you—not against you.

When I left my last "official job" to go all in on my dreams, I had no clue as to how I would pay my bills or how things would work out. I just knew that it was time; if I never took the leap to create the life of my dreams to be a full-time author and speaker, it would never happen. So I went completely all in at that point and haven't turned back since. There was a peace in me, deep down, in which I knew that all would work out. I didn't know exactly how, but I trusted in the process. Several weeks after I took the leap, I received a random email from a program manager who wanted to buy a large quantity of my first book, *You*. I had no idea that email was coming when I stepped into the unknown, but it did, and it happened because I put myself in the position to let it happen. This is just one of the many stories of how opportunities have presented themselves in their perfect times on my pursuit so far. I assure you, they will happen for you too. Trust in it.

When you are investing in your dreams with your time, talents, and resources, things will work out for you when you least expect them to. Doors will open and momentum will pick up. Your dreams will be supported, because you are putting the energy into making them happen. As you experience progress, random opportunities coming to you, and glimpses of your dreams being realized, you will gain more trust in the process.

There are no short cuts and no free passes. Overnight successes are not likely (they are rare, and oftentimes if they do happen, they don't last). There is a process to getting to where you deserve to be—living your dreams. It's not always pretty or easy, but if you keep taking action and trusting in your dreams, no matter how hard it gets or long it takes, eventually they will be realized. It may not happen on your terms, but it will happen.

PATIENCE

As I mentioned in the previous section, I thought that everything would just happen after my first book was published. I had not thought it would take so many years before living my dream appeared, even a little bit, as my efforts were gaining momentum and support. In other words, it was at least eight years or more before I saw even a glimpse of my dream, to inspire others through my books and speaking engagements full-time, being realized. I would get little bits of confirmation of my dreams becoming my reality, just enough to keep me going. The main thing

I had to rely on day after day is my belief, trust in the process, and patience. To keep believing, trusting, and waiting on something that was not yet realized, and certainly not promised, was not easy at all.

There were so many times that I just wanted it all to come together, and not only did I want it to, but I needed it to happen. In fact, there was a period in the process in which I only had thirty-seven dollars to my name. What made it scary was the fact that during the same time, my home was being foreclosed on. It felt like I was losing it all. I didn't have much time before I would eventually have to vacate my home and find a new place to live, which I didn't have the money to do. This was a stressful and terrifying time, but deep down I knew it would all work out. It had to!

When things seemed to get harder, I told myself that I would go as far as I needed to in order to make my dreams a reality. I will not stop for anything. I never imagined that it would come down to me having so little money to my name and being on the verge of not having a home to live in... homeless. The experience of losing my house and not having enough money to get into a new place to live challenged me on many levels. I was being tested to my core. If there was a time to give up on my dreams, it was then. I thought for sure that I would have way more traction than I did at that time, but I didn't. There seemed to be no relief in sight, but I moved through it, one step and one day at a time. I kept showing up and taking daily actions on my dreams, no matter what.

Finally, a completely unexpected thing happened. I got a random text from a woman that told me about an apartment she may be putting up for rent, months prior. She asked if I was still interested in renting her apartment. Knowing I didn't have any money to move in, I stepped through the door of opportunity anyway and said, "Sure, when can I see it?" When I showed up at the apartment, I quickly saw that it was run down. She started to tell me about the work she needed to have done before I could move in and about how long it would take before it was ready. The next thing I knew, I was saying, "I can do the work if you want to figure out a trade." We talked about everything in more detail, and she agreed to let me do it in exchange for my deposit and first month's rent. The work I did, with the help of a great friend, actually earned me several months of rent. It was amazing! I had to rise to the occasion to buy myself more time in the pursuit of my dreams, so I did.

It felt like I had a huge weight lifted off of my back, and I could focus again. The circumstance as a whole was quite humbling for me, but at the same time, it was inspiring. It strengthened my belief in my dreams and my ability to make them into my reality.

Although I would have much rather not have been in that situation in the first place, it was all a part of the process and worked out better than I ever could have imagined. Things will not always make sense or happen when you want them to, but if you keep trusting the process, are patient, and hang in there long enough—things have a way of working out.

There were months that lead up to this moment. I knew the foreclosure was happening. Even though I was slightly freaking out at the time, deep down, I kept believing that something would work out. It didn't happen like I thought it would or when I wanted it to, but in the end, it all worked out perfectly, within the exact time needed.

It is important to have patience while you're waiting for things to come together. There will be times when nothing seems to be working out and everything is crumbling down around you. Lean into your belief, keep working, trust, and be patient as the days unravel. Everything will eventually come together for you. Random opportunities will present themselves when you need them most. They will not always happen on your timeline or in the exact way you want them to, but they will happen. If you are willing, make the necessary sacrifices, stay devoted, are clear, work hard, and remain committed and courageous, then your dreams will become your reality.

STRUGGLE

Oftentimes, the conversation about how much of a struggle it is to manifest your dreams into reality is downplayed. There is general mention of them in stories about how different celebrities, musicians, and athletes overcame their struggles in order to achieve their dreams, which can be inspiring. Unfortunately, people tend to overlook the depth of their struggle, and what it has to teach. Instead, they fixate on their level of success. We want to hear more about what people have versus what they did, and had to go through, in order to get it.

There is a commonly shared story about the Hollywood Superstar Sylvester Stallone, right before his dreams started to manifest. One of his lowest points in his pursuit was when he had to sell his loyal companion, his dog, to a stranger outside of a liquor store, because he couldn't afford to feed it. He sold it for twenty-five dollars. I can only imagine how devastating that was. It didn't stop him though. He kept going. Not too long after that horrible experience, he wrote the script for the Oscar Award winning film, *Rocky*. Not only did he sell the script, he starred in the film. He eventually ended up finding the guy he sold his dog to and bought it back for fifteen thousand dollars. No matter how much Sylvester Stallone struggled, he never let it stop him from making his dreams a reality.

In the pursuit of your dreams, you will do more than struggle with finances. You will likely struggle with insecurities, failures, setbacks, obstacles, mistakes, confusion, frustration, and bouts with depression. The pathway to your dreams is not, and will not be, a straightforward path lined with sunshine and rainbows gently leading you to your dreams. Your dreams will not just happen because you decide to pursue them. You will struggle. In fact, you will struggle more than you may ever expect to. This is not good or bad; it's just a part of what it takes.

One of the great things about stories like Sylvester Stallone's, and the struggles that so many others went through before their dreams became reality, is that he didn't give up. The only reason you know about these stories is because the people had struggled as long as it took in order to make their dreams a reality. There is no specific time limit to how long you will or will not struggle. The duration is different for everyone. The ones who make their dreams a reality are the ones that keep pushing through their struggles, no matter how bad the struggles are or how long they last. They keep believing in, and acting on, their dreams until they come to be—no matter what.

None of this is to say that you will reach a major dream or goal and you will never struggle again. That is not the case at all. Chances are that you will always have something you are reaching for and working toward. Every great thing—including living the life of your dreams—comes from the ability to persevere through whatever struggles you face in order to achieve it.

Think of the struggles you encounter, and will encounter, as a necessary part of getting something that you really want. If you acknowledge that this is an unavoidable part of being able to live the life of your dreams, pushing through your struggles will be much easier.

As I mentioned before, I never expected any of this process to be so hard, and I believed that things would work out much faster and easier than they have. Getting through the struggles I had in order to be where I am today was worth it. I would go through every one of them again and again in order to experience the joy and fulfillment I have now from living my dreams to the extent I currently am.

There will be many highlights on the journey to your dreams. It will not be all struggles without any glimpses or experiences of reward and progress along the way. You will get moments of renewed inspiration and drive at the perfect times—when you need them most. There will always be reminders that bring you back to why you are facing obstacles and struggles in the first place, which is to live the life of your dreams. I always get an inspiring email, message, or comment from someone I inspired in the times when I feel discouraged. They always come at just the right time and keep me connected to the drive I need to continue living the life of my dreams. I am always so grateful when these reminders come.

As tempting and easy as it may seem to be, don't give up on your dreams. You deserve to make them your reality. When you are in the midst of struggles, don't ever see them as a sign that you should choose an easier direction than following your dreams. Take the struggles you will encounter, or may be encountering right now, for what they are—a part of what it will take for you to make your dreams a reality. You don't have to resent them or let them stop you, just accept them and keep going. There is always a way to get through whatever struggle you face.

Keep your mind sharp and your eyes open for opportunities, support, and inspiration. Remind yourself of the many people who have already experienced great rewards from making it through the struggles they faced. Their dreams were realized because they kept rising above their challenges and didn't give up. Whatever you face will eventually pass. You will make it through. Stay up. Keep pushing, trusting, believing, and knowing that your greatest challenges and setbacks are a part of the process that is bringing you even closer to your dreams.

One day, you will be living the life of your dreams, and when that time comes, you will look back with appreciation for every struggle you went through to get there. It's all worth it!

SELF-CARE

If you commit your life fully to your dreams in order to make them your reality, it is important that you take great care of yourself along the way. If you don't, the pursuit will be much harder than it already is, if not impossible. Becoming so focused on your goals and dreams that you stop taking the time to take care of yourself is easy. This often happens when you have momentum, and your dreams continue to demand more of your time, attention, and energy. When you neglect your self-care, you create burnout, fatigue, depression, anxiety, and complacency. When you take care of yourself, you are less likely to burn out, get tired, and become depressed. You are more grounded and better able to manage anxiety, as well as be inspired with action, when you take good care of yourself. Not only are you a better version of yourself because of it, but you are also able to give more fully to your dreams.

Find things that help you stay inspired, and if you already have them, keep doing them. If you want to create the life of your dreams, then you will need to take care of yourself first. Self-care must be a part of your daily routine. Orchestrate your days in such a way that taking care of yourself and doing things that help you stay inspired is part of them. Self-care not only helps you feel good; it makes you a better person for the world around you, and especially for being ready to achieve your dreams.

I get it; it's not always easy to make time to take care of yourself. I respect if you feel guilty doing so and you think it is much more productive if you spend that extra time acting on your dreams instead of taking care of yourself. However, when you're inspired and energized, the action time you do spend on your dreams is more effective and productive.

Making your dreams a reality is not a sprint—it's a

marathon. You have to pace yourself, regardless of how much noise is out there that says, "It's all about the grind." It is a grind; your dreams do require a lot of hard work and most of your time and attention. However, if you don't do the things that help you sustain your focus, passion, and drive in the process of reaching your dreams, you will not make it.

When striving toward your dreams, you can be as busy as you want. Yet if the work you're doing isn't of high quality, then it's not going to move the needle much at all. Make taking great care of yourself a priority. Don't waiver from it, not for anyone or anything. Your dreams depend on it!

STAY IN YOUR LANE

Once you are clear on your focus, stay in your lane. Do not get tempted to change lanes because one looks faster, easier, or appears to be the one that everyone else is taking. It is easy to see what others are doing and compare yourself with where they appear to be versus where you are. When it seems to be working for them, you feel like it should work for you too. If the path is authentic to you, really speaks to you, and will take you closer to realizing your dreams, then that's different. If that is the case, then go for it. However, don't do things because you think it will get you to where you're aspiring to go faster or easier. Don't get pulled out of your lane based on what others are doing... or are telling you that you should be doing.

Your path is unique to you and is not the same as anyone else's. The dreams you are pursuing, or will start pursuing, are yours and no one else's. Sure, people may be living the life of your dreams now for which you are aspiring to, but they will never be the exact same as what yours will be. The exact details of what someone else did, the lanes they say they traveled in to live their dreams, will be different for everyone. Do what is right for you, and let others do what works for them.

I get the attraction of mimicking exactly what others are doing that you are inspired by, and even the pressure to follow their lead. I deal with this often and continuously have to bring myself back to the truth of my own journey. Just because another author is offering online courses doesn't mean that I have to. If that does not speak to me, at least not at this point, then taking action in that direction will be more of a detour than it would be something that contributes to me living my dreams to the fullest. It will not bring me closer, but instead take me further away. It is especially difficult to avoid being distracted from your path when you see—or at least when you are shown on social media—how "successful" different paths appear to be for others.

Making your dreams a reality is not always about what others call success, at least not society's outward depictions and acknowledgments of it. Although one cannot deny the appeal and enjoyment of what they see, ultimately, following your dreams is about fulfillment. The more you stand in your truth and stay in your lane, the more fulfilling your life will become. Honor the experiences, decisions, actions, and bursts of inspirations that feel authentic to you. They are the voices of your dreams calling you. The things that keep you driven and excited, no matter who sees them, how many "likes" you get, or how much money you earn, are the ones that will make the life of your dreams into a reality. Act on them with all of your heart, and forget the rest.

CLOSING THOUGHTS

Following your dreams is one of the most difficult things you will ever do. On the other hand, making your dreams into your reality is one of the most rewarding and worthwhile pursuits of your life.